THE BLOOD OF JESUS AS A WEAPON

Pastor Uzor Ndekwu

THE BLOOD OF JESUS AS A WEAPON

Pastor Uzor Ndekwu

MEMOIRS
Cirencester

United Kingdom:

Uzor Ndekwu Ministries (Jesus Sanctuary)
25/27 Ruby Street
Old Kent Road
London SE15 1LR
United Kingdom
Tel: +44 207 277 5664; +44 7961 276 187
Email: info@jesussanctuaryministries.org
Website: www.jesussanctuaryministries.org

Nigeria:

Uzor Ndekwu Ministries (Jesus Sanctuary)
41 Otigba Crescent
GRA
Onitsha
Anambra State
Nigeria
Te: +234 803 395 0197; +234 803 405 2113

Published by:

Uzor Ndekwu Ministries (Jesus Sanctuary)

Bible quotations are from the King James Version of the Holy Bible.

Printed by

Memoirs Publishers
England

ISBN 978-1-908223-65-4

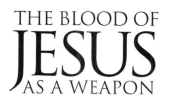

THE BLOOD OF
JESUS
AS A WEAPON

CONTENTS: Page

ACKNOWLEDGEMENTS

I wish to express my profound thanks to the following persons: my wife for her help and support and for checking and editing the original draft, Pastor Obi (Pastor of Jesus Sanctuary Ministries, Onitsha Branch) for the insightful testimonies, Dr Osakwe Chinweuba (the former occultist who gave his life to Christ and is now a Minister of God) for his powerful insights into the activities of occultic people using the Heavenlies, Brother Andrew Onwuemene, who typed the original manuscript, and Mr Chris Newton for the editing and proof-reading of the book.

CHAPTER 1 - INTRODUCTION

In most matters, the spiritual and physical realms are opposed to each other, because their origins, functions, occupants and dynamics differ. What works in the spiritual realm may not necessarily work in the physical realm, because the spiritual world is basically for the unseen, the immaterial and the invisible, and the laws that govern it are totally different from those that rule the physical world. The laws that operate in the spiritual realm are universal, because the spiritual realm is one entity and operates under one divine sovereignty. For example, the law of giving (sowing and reaping) is a universal principle which knows no boundary.

In the physical realm it is a different story, because it is for the visible, the material and the carnal, and the rules of engagement are different. This is because the laws that govern the physical realm are subject to different historical, social, cultural and moral imperatives.

For example, constitutional, currency and cultural imperatives differ from nation to nation because nations are made up of different people and concepts of right and wrong depend on different social, cultural, moral and value foundations. What may be morally wrong in one country may be acceptable in another. Basically, therefore, the physical and the spiritual realms are contrary to one another.

Because the things that are not seen are eternal, while the things that are seen are temporal (2 Corinthians 4:18). There is rarely a common ground between the two realms. However, it is in the blood issue that the two realms (spiritual and physical) appear to be in agreement. Both realms understand and appreciate and depend on the blood as a vital life-line.

THE PHYSICAL REALM

The importance of the blood to all living creatures cannot be over-emphasised. Physically, most living creatures depend on blood for their growth, nourishment and survival. Blood holds and sustains the organs of the body and without it the body would cease to function.

Even the scripture emphasises the importance of the blood to the body. It is stated that the life of the flesh is in the blood (Leviticus 17:11). The blood, therefore, is like the petrol that drives the engine of the body. Scientifically, the practice of medicine has benefited hugely from blood tests and transfusion programmes which have helped immensely in the fight against deadly and terminal diseases. This has contributed to the development and advancement of mankind in general. So the blood is important to the physical aspect of man and his environment.

THE SPIRITUAL REALM

Just as the blood is important to the physical world, the blood is equally vital to the spiritual one. The foundation, fundamentals and dynamism of the spirit realm are determined by the blood – whether it is the blood of all living creatures, the fowls of the air and creeping things, or the Blood of Jesus Christ. According to the scriptures:

"... if the blood of bulls and of goats, and the ashes of an heifer sprinkling the unclean, sanctifieth to the purifying of the flesh: How much more shall the blood of Christ, who through the eternal Spirit offered himself without spot to God, purge your conscience from dead works to serve the living God?" (Hebrew 9:13-14).

What the scripture is saying is that blood is blood, and no matter what its source, it has its own spiritual potency. However, the Blood of Jesus Christ is superior and all-encompassing, and therefore effective both physically and spiritually. The blood, therefore, is the vital link between the invisible and the invisible; between the invisible and the visible; between God and man, and between man and man. Without the blood, there would be no relationship, contact or connection between the two realms. That is why the foundations of the Old and New Testaments were based on the blood. In the Old Testament, God used animals blood to lay the foundation, while in the New Testament, the Blood of Jesus was offered as a substitutionary platform.

THE OLD TESTAMENT

The Old Testament actually began in the Garden of Eden, and the need for it came as a result of sin. If Adam and Eve had not failed God, there would have been no need for a testament. The foundation of the Old Testament began when God killed some animals and used coats of their skins to cover Adam and Eve's nakedness. This act by God, which necessitated the sacrifice of animals and the blood spills therefrom, activated the Law of Substitution, in a limited sense. The animals that were killed by God in order to obtain the coats of skins took the place of Adam and Eve that sinned. They ought to have paid the ultimate penalty, because God had earlier commanded

"... in the day that you eatest thereof thou shalt surely die" (Genesis 2:17).

The commandment was clearly addressed to Adam, but when they eventually ate the fruit of the tree of the knowledge of good and evil, it was the animals that paid with their lives, to cover Adam and Eve's nakedness. Thus was laid the groundwork of the Old Testament. And the blood of animals became the platform for a covenant relationship between God and man (Exodus 24:6-8). As a result, all the provisions and blessings of God became accessible only through blood sacrifice. For example, those desiring healing and cleansing, (Leviticus 14:4-6); sin offering (Leviticus 8:14-15); protection and guidance (Exodus 12:12-14), and altar foundation (2 Kings 16:15 and 2 Chronicles 29:22) all involved sacrifices.

The kinds of animals or birds to be used

depended largely on the intent and purpose of the sacrifice. Thus the Old Testament foundation was based on sacrificial imperatives, which was begun by God. Contrary to popular belief, Moses did not begin the Old Testament but institutionalised it. And when he needed to seal the commandments of God with the people, he used the sacrificed blood of oxen by taking

> *"... half of the blood, and... sprinkled on the altar. And he took the book of the covenant, and read in the audience of the people: and they said, All that the Lord hath said, we will do, and be obedient. And Moses took the blood, and sprinkled it on the people, and said, Behold the blood of the covenant, which the Lord hath made concerning all these words."* (Exodus 24:6-8).

This act performed by Moses applied also to other Patriarchs who were in covenant relationships with God, e.g. Abraham, Isaac and

Jacob. For the sake of emphasis, when Abraham wanted to seal up the covenant between God and himself, God told him to:

"...Take me an heifer of three years old, and a she goat of three years old, and a ram of three years old, and a turtledove, and a young pigeon" (Genesis 15:9)

for sacrifice. It is clear that they all took the pattern of God as practised in the Garden of Eden. Therefore, one can say that Moses did not begin the Old Testament; he only institutionalized it. When God sacrificed some animals to cover Adam and Eve's sin, the foundation of the Old Testament was laid.

Be that as it may, in spite of the blood foundation, the Old Testament lacked the redemptive capacity to deliver the soul of man from the powers of darkness. Sin and death still have overwhelming dominion over man. This is because, the blood of bulls, goats, birds and calves could only provide for the flesh. That blood was to make atonement for the sin of the flesh, for example, when someone commits sins of adultery or stealing.

The blood foundation of the Old Testament was never instituted to deliver man. It was fundamentally incapacitated. It was only meant to cover the nakedness of mankind, because the animals that were killed by God could not have been an appropriate substitute for Adam and Eve's sin and the consequences of eternal death. It only covered their nakedness (Genesis 3:21). To expect otherwise would have been impossible in the realm of equity, because Adam and Eve who sinned were not of equal value to the animals that were sacrificed. The Old Testament was essentially inadequate and limited for redemption purposes, hence the need for a new covenant to address the inadequacies of the old.

THE NEW TESTAMENT

From the substitutionary perspective, it is the death and Blood of Jesus Christ that brought equity in the realm of exchange. For if the disobedience and sin of Adam and Eve brought sin and death upon the human race, the obedience and death of Jesus Christ on the Cross of Calvary brought righteousness and eternal life to mankind. As Apostle Paul graphically stated:

"For if by one man's offence death reigned by one; much more they which receive abundance of grace and of the gift of righteousness shall reign in life by one, Jesus Christ.) Therefore as by the offence of one judgment came upon all men to condemnation; even so by the righteousness of one the free gift came upon all men unto justification of life. For as by one man's disobedience many were made sinners, so by the obedience of one shall many be made righteous." (Romans 5:17-19).

So the New Testament was designed and orchestrated by God to redeem mankind through the covenant blood of Jesus Christ. It is God who gave His Son to die for our sins. As Apostle John said:

"For God so loved the world, that he gave his only begotten Son, that whosoever believeth in him should not perish, but have everlasting life.
(John 3:16).

The blood of Jesus, as the chief cornerstone of the New Testament, was designed as a comprehensive redemption package for mankind. Mankind was given a better and superior platform to access and appropriate the full benefits of the blood in redeeming ourselves from the powers of darkness.

It has provided full opportunity for reconciliation between God and His children. As Apostle Paul noted:

"But Christ being come an high priest of good things to come, by a greater and more perfect tabernacle, not made with hands, that is to say, not of this building; (12) Neither by the blood of goats and calves, but by his own blood he entered in once into the holy place, having

obtained eternal redemption for us. (13) For if the blood of bulls and of goats, and the ashes of an heifer sprinkling the unclean, sanctifieth to the purifying of the flesh: (14) How much more shall the blood of Christ, who through the eternal Spirit offered himself without spot to God..." (Hebrews 9:11-14).

Simply put, the blood of Jesus was meant to give us full and complete freedom, salvation, protection and rest from the powers of darkness. However, many children of God are still suffering from satanic manipulations, oppression, possession and suppression. Although the blood of Jesus was made available over 2000 years ago, most people have not realized that there are issues and circumstances that you need to overcome with the application of the blood of Jesus. From the confessions of some native doctors and men of the occult that Jesus touched through our television programmes, the use of animal and bird blood for satanic and demonic activities are quite prevalent. According to them, most spells, incantations, divinations and enchantments are energized through the use of the blood of living creatures, and the kind of creature used depends on their intent or purpose.

The implication is that it is only with the superior blood of Jesus Christ that you can undo the works of darkness. As earlier said, the covenant relationship between the invisible and the visible is based on the sacrificial system, through the blood (in Old Testament times by the blood of living creatures, and in New Testament times by the blood of Jesus Christ). Therefore, whenever people want to connect heaven and earth, visible and invisible, God and man, it must be through the blood. When Abraham wanted to guarantee his inheritance, he sacrificed to God (Genesis 15:7-9). And because of the sacrifice, God made a covenant with Abraham that to his seed he would give the land from the River Euphrates to the people of the Kenites, Kenizzites, Kadmonites, Hittites, Perizzites, Rephaims, Amorites, Canaanites,

Girgashites and Jebusites. Subsequently, when Abraham attempted to sacrifice his son Isaac, God told Abraham:

> *"By myself have I sworn, saith the Lord, for because thou hast done this thing, and hast not withheld thy son, thine only son: That in blessing I will bless thee, and in multiplying I will multiply thy seed as the stars of the heaven, and as the sand which is upon the sea shore; and thy seed shall possess the gate of his enemies."* (Genesis 22:16-17).

Just as money is the currency of the physical realm, the blood is the currency of the spiritual realm. From the negative perspective, when the King of Moab desperately wanted the war to turn against the Israelites,

> *"... he took with him seven hundred men that drew swords, to break through even unto the king of Edom: but they could not. Then he took his eldest son that should have reigned in his stead,*

and offered him for a burnt offering upon the wall. And there was great indignation against Israel: and they departed from him, and returned to their own land." (2 Kings 3:26-27).

This negative act by the King of Moab has made some people, especially those in the occult world, use their children, wives, husbands or other relatives for ritual purposes to achieve their devilish goals or objectives.

The use of human blood for satanic sacrifices is prevalent in our societies. The church has failed to confront these practices because satanic groups have penetrated its ranks. Because of the financial contributions of their members, they have succeeded in derailing the spiritual fervency of the churches. The church of Christ has become not only worldly, but instrumental in polluting the children of God through perverted teachings.

The love of money, which is the theology of Satan, is now actively propagated in the evangelical churches as well. The redemption and care for souls to be delivered from the powers of darkness has taken a lower priority. It is not surprising that though Christian activities have increased in our generation, occultic practices have taken a much bigger leap. What used to be 'secret societies' are now openly called occultic groups, and they practise their demonic activities for all and sundry to notice and be enticed. Their activities are so prevalent that our children in secondary and tertiary institutions are being initiated, and most of these initiations in schools are done with animal and human blood.

These children do not understand the implications of their involvement. The scripture forbids eating or drinking of blood. God, through Moses, told the children of Israel:

".......Ye shall eat the blood of no manner of flesh: for the life of all flesh is the blood thereof: whosoever eateth it shall be cut off." (Leviticus 17:14).

It is therefore wrong to drink or taste any human or animal blood as practised in the occultic world, because it is a mortal sin against God.

Some people drink human blood without knowing that they have committed a mortal sin against God. Beside the occult practices, we have handled cases of infatuated lovers who ignorantly drank or tasted the blood of each other under oath. This act destroys the future and happiness of those who indulge in it, and deliverances of such people are quite difficult. These case studies illustrate this issue clearly:

CHAPTER 2 - CASE STUDIES

CASE STUDY 1: THE SACRIFICE

Peter, Ogonna, Chike and Augustine (not their real names) were in one of the cult groups in university. Part of their initiation involved sacrificing a disabled boy. The killing could not be officially traced to them because the school authorities were also living in fear of the group. However, all these boys eventually died in one strange circumstance or the other. Peter became mentally ill and died on a rubbish heap. Ogonna and Augustine died in a fatal motor accident, while Chike was kidnapped and never found.

CASE STUDY 2: THE BROKEN COVENANT

The case of Emeka and Janet (not their real names) is instructive. Emeka was a welder and was doing well financially, while Janet was exceptionally beautiful and intelligent but from a poor home. Because of her poor financial background, there was an informal agreement for Emeka to train her as his future wife. When the girl was in the first year of university, she decided she would not go ahead with that arrangement and her parents offered to pay back to Emeka whatever expenses he had incurred. However, Emeka refused. The matter was complicated, because both of them had used blood as a covenant. When they came to see me, it was very obvious there was a wide gap in physical appearance between the man and the girl. Even when the church offered to pay additional money to Emeka to appeal to him to break the covenant, still he refused. In such circumstances you need the full co-operation of both parties, since blood is involved.

CASE STUDY 3: THE SECRET COVENANT

Chinyere entered into a blood covenant with her boyfriend when she was a youth, promising each other that they would eventually marry. During her Youth Service she met a very rich man who swept her off her feet and caused her to dump her covenanted boyfriend. After the wedding, the man she married became mentally ill and lost most of his wealth. Chinyere has been unable to conceive, despite medical assurances that she and her husband were able to have children. Because of the suspicious in-laws, they decided to go to the diviners. This caused her to confess that she was covenanted by blood to another man. We see this principle in the bible regarding Abraham and Abimelech in Genesis 20:2-7, 17-18

> *"... And Abimelech King of Gerar sent, and took Sarah. But God came to Abimelech in a dream by night, and said to him, Behold, thou art but a dead man, for the woman which thou hast taken; for she is a man's wife... Now therefore restore the man his wife ... And if thou restore her not, know thou that thou shalt surely die... and God healed Abimelech, and his wife... For the LORD had fast closed up all the wombs of the house of Abimelech."*

Even though Abimelech was not a party to the deception of Abraham, he still suffered and barrenness came to his household. Though Chinyere's husband was ignorant of the blood covenant, they both suffered the consequences. In the realm of the spirit Chinyere belonged to another man, whether he was aware of it or not.

CASE STUDY 4: A CRIPPLED BUSINESS AND MARRIAGE

Mark met my wife for counselling, complaining of financial problems and stagnation in his business. He said his wife of three years was unable to conceive, although there was no medical reason for this. He also complained that his former girlfriend kept threatening him and his wife. My wife asked a couple of questions and realized from his answers that the man was in blood covenant with his former girlfriend. According to him the covenant had not been broken, because his former girlfriend still wanted them to marry, but he did not want to marry her, because, in his words, "she was too short".

CHAPTER 3

ANIMAL BLOOD SACRIFICES

Apart from the personal negative consequences that befall those who use blood for their selfish ends, many satanic agents and evil persons have employed the blood of different animals or birds to hinder the success or progress of their victims. I will summarize the potential effects of the blood of each animal or bird, as stated by Dr Chinweuba (the former occultic practitioner who is now a Minister of God):

■ 1. BLOOD OF GOATS

Like the blood of human beings, goat blood is used by the wicked ones to raise altars to hinder the progress of a building or a project. Timothy decided to build a bungalow in his home town. Traditionally, when one takes up a building project, the elders of the town are invited to "pray" over the land, which (among other things) they do by sacrificing goats. However, the sacrifice ends up working against both the project and the individual. This is what happened to Timothy. Shortly after the elders performed their blood sacrifice, he lost his lucrative job. It became a struggle to finish the house. Thirty years later, the house, though plastered and roofed, still has no windows or doors apart from one room. It is neither connected to electricity nor painted.

■ 2. BLOOD OF MALE GOATS, LIZARDS AND VULTURES

The blood of male goats, lizards and vultures, laced with incantations, are used to project rejection. When any of these types of blood are used to energize a curse against someone, they experience rejection, no matter how nice they try to be. Some people find that those that they have helped previously turn against them; others discovered that their bosses hate them for no obvious reasons, while traders may find no one wants to patronize their business or enter their shop.

A successful businesswoman gave a testimony concerning her business. One day when she opened her shop, a number of lizards came running out. She wondered how they had come to be in her shop, but did not give it a second thought. However, from that day on, no customer ever entered her shop again, and she had to close through lack of sales. After hearing the teaching of the effects of lizards in church, she prayed with the prayer points and things were restored back to normal.

Another lady, Mercy, spoke about how her once-loving husband had turned against her and begun to show her disdain and hatred. He sometimes complained that she had an offensive odour, and said that although she used all sorts of deodorants and perfumes, she still smelt like a male goat. After hearing the teaching about lizards, male goats and vultures, she used the prayer points and their marriage was restored.

■ 3. BLOOD OF SNAKES

Snake blood is used to project lust. In Genesis

3:1-8, it was a serpent that Satan worked through to project lust (lust of the eyes and lust of the flesh) into Eve: Genesis 3:4-6: *"Ye shall not surely die... And when the woman saw that the tree was good for food, and that it was pleasant to the eyes... She took of the fruit thereof."* Most prostitutes use snake blood to bath and project lust against their intended victims (their clients). Also most stage performers and people who are involved in pornographic activities use such blood to bath for group attractions and effects. It is no coincidence that pictures of live pythons are commonly used in advertisements for cars, clothing and boutiques, to mention but a few.

■ 4. BLOOD OF RAMS AND SHEEP

Rams' blood is often used to induce new demonic energy and strength. Charms and amulets energized with it activate much havoc and destruction upon their victims. Conversely, most native doctors and satanic agents shed such blood to celebrate "victory" or "success" after the satanic performance of destructive contracts or assignments. Rams' blood is also used to revalidate or energise an idol or shrine for increased strength in satanic activation.

With sheep, because of their calm and non-violent nature, their blood is used to cast spells on people in order to control a man or woman by making them docile and sheepish. The victim of such spells will never question the activities of their spouses. One woman, Mrs WK, confessed that her friend had deceived her into using such charms on her husband. After a while, the man's relations succeeded in bringing the man for counselling. The woman, under the influence of the Holy Spirit, then began to confess all her nefarious activities. Although we later prayed for her, the man's family never agreed to any settlement, because the children were from other men.

■ 5. BLOOD OF WHITE AND BLACK COCKS AND OTHERS

Most marine agents use the blood of white or black hens for satanic sacrifices and appeasement. According to the self-confessed marine witchdoctor who challenged us and later got converted in Onitsha, Nigeria, if you want the marine spirit/satanic visitation, the blood of a white cock is required for a demonic bath and purification. You can demand "blessings" from the water kingdom after the necessary rituals, and such blessings manifest immediately. But to ensure the continuity of the blessings, they often use infant blood. One can therefore surmize that this is the reason why Pharaoh commanded that the Hebrew children should be killed by the midwives, and when the midwives failed to comply, the male children were to be thrown into the river:

"And the King of Egypt spake to the Hebrew midwives, of which... and Pharaoh charged all his people, saying, Every son that is born you shall cast into the river, and every daughter ye shall save alive" (Exodus 1:15-22).

■ 6. BLOOD OF CHICKS

The blood of chicks is used to project accidents

and violent deaths. When evil people want to do this they make a sacrifice, calling the name of their intended victims, and violently pull the chick's head off from the body, using the blood to seal the sacrifice. A case in point is a family of 4 who all died through motor accidents.

CHAPTER 4

HUMAN SACRIFICES

Human blood has been used for satanic sacrifices and activities through the ages, though the scriptures condemn such demonic actions. The Psalmist said:

> *"And they served their idols: which were a snare unto them. Yea, they sacrificed their sons and their daughters unto devils, And shed innocent blood, even the blood of their sons and of their daughters, whom they sacrificed unto the idols of Canaan: and the land was polluted with blood."* (Psalms 106:36-38).

It is amazing that in our time and age, with Christianity and the Word of God so widespread, some people still indulge in such dastardly acts.

Because of the perverted belief that men are givers of life and that life is in the blood, and that it is the man that determines the blood group of a child, some evil men use the blood of men for sacrifice in order to prolong their own life. It is believed that those in occult and other dark societies use the blood of men to exchange for more years of life for themselves. This is the negative law of evil substitution, which is a corruption of God's law of substitution. According to the scripture:

"The wicked shall be a ransom for the righteous, and the transgressor for the upright." (Proverbs 21:18).

What the wicked people are doing is to turn this Word of God upside down. In practice, weak victims, relations, friends, in-laws, etc are used for satanic substitution. There are families where the deaths of promising young men are yearly occurrences. The "strongman" in that family may be short-changing the lives of these young men for their demonic agenda. That is why the scripture says that unless you bind the strongman, he will spoil your goods (Matthew 12:29). The subsequent chapters will expose and teach you how to paralyse the strongman that is against your future.

On the other hand, women are the source of blessings, as mentioned by the scriptures:

"Whoso findeth a wife findeth a good thing, and obtaineth favour of the Lord." (Proverbs 18:22).

Some wicked and evil people even use the blood of their wives, mothers and daughters to attract wealth. It is surprising in our age and time, given the level of civilization and religious awareness, that such satanic activities are so prevalent. What is particularly surprising and shocking is that such despicable and ungodly acts are mentioned among the so-called evangelical and pentecostal churches. That is why the churches are disconnected from God and the people. When they spread their hands to God He will not see them, and when they pray, He will not hear, for their hands are full of blood (Isaiah 1:15). However, God assured Isaiah that all wicked oppressors shall be drunken with their own blood (Isaiah 49:26). And for God, all those who shed innocent blood shall be pursued by blood (Ezekiel 35:6). As children of God, the only effective way to resist oppressors, evil men and women, occultic people and the practitioners of demonic rituals is to invoke the Covenant of Exemption and to activate the Law of Substitution.

CHAPTER 5

THE COVENANT OF EXEMPTION

Generally, the Covenant of Exemption is anchored in the blood. The blood is a sort of spiritual insurance cover. In the Old Testament, the use of human and animal blood for such covenant activities was prevalent. The blood does provide limited cover. For example, when the children of Israel were to leave the land of Egypt and the Angel of Death was to execute judgement, those who had the blood on their doorposts escaped:

> *"Speak ye unto all the congregation of Israel, saying, In the tenth day of this month they shall take to them every man a lamb, according to the house of their fathers, a lamb for an house: ...shall take it out from the sheep, or from the goats: ...And they shall take of the blood, and strike it on the two side posts and on the upper door post of the houses... For I will pass through the land of Egypt this night,*

and smite all the firstborn in the land of Egypt, both man and beast; and against all the gods of Egypt I will execute judgment: I am the Lord. And the blood shall be to you for a token upon the houses where ye are: and when I see the blood, I will pass over you, and the plague shall not be upon you to destroy you, when I smite the land of Egypt" (Exodus 12:3-13).

It is surprising, in this era of the New Testament where such animal sacrifices are not necessary because of the exemption it gives, that people still use animal blood for covenants of exemption which do not work. The case of Mr Okafor (not his real name) is a good example. According to him, he went to a native doctor for a covenant of exemption from accidents as a preventive measure. This was after the death of a close friend. He took the advice of some of his friends to prepare charms for exemption from accident, so that he would not die before his time. However, he noticed three months later that he kept having accidents, although he never got injured. The incidents became a weekly occurrence, so he came to the church. He brought a charm energized with animal blood, which we destroyed. This was because the Old Testament Covenant of Exemption principle activated by the native doctor was fundamentally limited. There was no redemptive provision. The Old Testament was not instituted for man's redemption but to cover the nakedness of sin. In effect, Mr Okafor had a fake spiritual insurance policy.

However, in the New Testament, the Covenant of Exemption is anchored in the Blood of Jesus Christ. The Blood of our Lord Jesus Christ is effective because the Mediator of the New Testament was superior to man and therefore His blood was more than adequate for man's redemption. Once you are born again and live by the word of God, you are automatically connected to the blood of Jesus Christ. This is because you were originally purchased by the blood of Jesus (Acts 20:28). You are therefore redeemed from being a prey to the powers of darkness, because the scripture says:

> *"they overcame by the blood of the lamb...."* (Revelation 12:11a).

The only way one can effectively overcome the agents of darkness is through the blood of Jesus Christ. As noted by Apostle Paul:

> *"in whom we have redemption through His blood (Jesus Christ) the forgiveness of sins, according to the riches of His grace."* (Ephesians 1:7).

The blood of Jesus perfected the inadequacy that was in the blood of bulls, goats, birds, and human beings. According to the scripture,

> *"For (if) the blood of bulls and goats, and the ashes of an heifer sprinkling the unclean, sanctifieth to the purifying of the flesh"* (Hebrews 9:13).

"For a testament is of force after men are dead: otherwise it is of no strength at all while the testator liveth" (Hebrews 9:15-17). And once Jesus arose from the grave with the keys of King David, the power of the grave was conquered, and man's ability to deal with agents of death was established. So the power of death lost its hold on man:

> *"For since by man came death, by man came also the resurrection of the dead."*
> (1 Corinthians 15:21).

Just as in Adam all died, and the covenant of death was established, also in Christ Jesus, all will be made alive and covenant of life instituted. Accordingly, death lost its sting and the grave was dispossessed of its victory. And those who know their authority in the Blood and Name of Jesus can never die before their time. One can therefore invoke the Covenant of Exemption using the power and authority in the Blood and Name of Jesus Christ to cast down evil imaginations and thoughts that are contrary to the will and purpose of God for your life. As the scripture says:

"(For the weapons of our warfare are not carnal, but mighty through God to the pulling down of strong holds;) (5) Casting down imaginations, and every high thing that exalteth itself against the knowledge of God, and bringing into captivity every thought to the obedience of Christ." (2 Corinthians 10:4-5).

Therefore, whenever thoughts of sickness, death, failure, shame, poverty or disasters come into your heart, reject them. And since death and life are in the power of the tongue (Proverbs 18:21), you are in a position to decree a thing and it shall be established in Jesus' Name (Job 22:28).

CHAPTER 6

THE LAW OF SUBSTITUTION

Unlike the Covenant of Exemption, which is based on the blood, the Law of Substitution is anchored in the blood and the power of the tongue. In this law, from the positive perspective, the stronger force uses the weaker force for substitution. For example, the Bible says the wicked shall be a ransom for the righteous (Proverbs 21:18). If you examine the lives of those who are righteous before God in the scriptures, instead of evil coming to them, that evil is automatically substituted. For example, most of David's enemies died for his sake. Another example is Mordecai and Haman. Whatever evil Haman planned for Mordecai, it was substituted and instead of Mordecai dying, Haman died.

> *"And the king arising from the banquet of wine in his wrath went into the palace garden: and Haman stood up to make request for his life to Esther the queen; for he saw that there was evil determined against him by the king... and Haman was*

fallen upon the bed whereon Esther was. Then said the king, Will he force the queen also before me in the house? As the word went out of the king's mouth, they covered Haman's face. And Harbonah, one of the chamberlains, said before the king, Behold also, the gallows fifty cubits high, which Haman had made for Mordecai, who had spoken good for the king, standeth in the house of Haman. Then the king said, Hang him thereon. So they hanged Haman on the gallows that he had prepared for Mordecai. Then was the king's wrath pacified."
(Esther 7:7-10).

These people know their God, and the power of the tongue (prophetic prayers or decrees). In the New Testament, this Law of Substitution is automatic for those who are covered by the Blood of Jesus Christ and understand the power of decreeing a thing so that they can be established:

"Thou shalt also decree a thing, and it shall be established unto thee: and the light shall shine upon thy ways." (Job 22:28)

and

> *"Verily I say unto you, Whatsoever ye shall bind on earth shall be bound in heaven: and whatsoever ye shall loose on earth shall be loosed in heaven."* (Matthew 18:18).

From the above scripture, all those who know their rights and position in the Lord and the knowledge of the Word of God should never fall victim to the evil imaginations of the wicked ones. According to the scripture, those who know their God shall be strong and do exploits (Daniel 11:32). Negatively, it is important to note that those in the occultic world equally apply this principle for their selfish ends. They substitute the lives or the stars of their victims for their own devilish purposes. The people who thrive in such evil manipulations use divinations, enchantments and demonic sacrifices which may involve human or animal blood. As usual, they use evil altars to execute their plans. In the scripture, the story of Balaam and Balak is very instructive. They raised seven altars in different locations in order to perform satanic sacrifices aimed at cursing those whom God had blessed, and the people to be cursed never knew what Balaam and Balak were executing against them (Numbers 23:1-18), neither did they offend Balaam and Balak. Therefore, people can come after you to destroy your destiny for no justifiable cause or reason.

In Acts 23:12, certain Jews bonded together and bound themselves under a curse, saying that they would neither drink nor eat till they had killed Paul. Apostle Paul was only a messenger of the Good News of our Lord Jesus Christ that delivered many from the powers of darkness. That is why Isaiah said:

> *"Woe unto them that decree unrighteous decrees, and that write grievousness which they have prescribed;"* (Isaiah 10:1).

Scripture says that surely there is no enchantment against (you), neither is there any divination against (your family members) that shall prosper (Numbers 23:23). One can therefore say that some family stagnations, individual frustrations, generational sickness and afflictions may be the result of secret demonic activities by the wicked ones assigned against them. From our counselling experiences over the years, the following signs, symptoms and manifestations may be direct consequences of evil and satanic blood sacrifices:

- **Untimely Physical Death** - Some experience a cycle of untimely death in their family. A lady spoke of how she lost her father, exactly a year later her elder brother died, and exactly a year after that her son died.

- **Relational Separation (Divorce)** - Blood forms a bond/covenant in marital relationships through sexual union; as a result blood is also used to destroy that bond and project divorce.

- **Emotional and Social** - Some people shut down from having contact with people.

- **Thoughts of Murder** - Some people have a lust for blood and must spill the blood of others. This bloodthirstiness is projected by evil blood sacrifice. The youth-on-youth knife crimes in the UK and the gang warfare in Mexico are examples of such.

- **Suicide** - Blood can be used to project

suicide. After people quarrel with a loved one or children are chastised, the thought can come on them to kill themselves.

■ **Miscarriage** - Careless disposal of sanitary pads can open the door to this form of attack. Evil people use menstrual blood to project barrenness and miscarriages in women who throw away used pads carelessly.

■ **Despondency** - Strong feeling of unhappiness or despair caused by difficulties which you feel you cannot overcome.

■ **Accidents** - Experiencing constant motor accidents. Blood sacrifices, especially of birds, are made at road junctions in order to promote accidents. Evil people monitor a person's route and make blood sacrifices to cause an accident. Some stretches of road are more accident-prone than others.

■ **Isolation** - The feeling of always being watched.

■ **Disillusionment** - Disappointment with something that turned out differently from what one expected, e.g. after marriage, people sometimes complain that their husband or wife is not what they expected.

- **Darkness of Mind** - Excessive fear and manipulation.
- **Violent Tendencies** - Violent films serve as an altar of violence because there is much blood-letting and many violent deaths. Many who watch such films tend to get possessed with violent spirits and thereafter become violent themselves.
- **Nightmares and Terror Experiences**
- **Excessive Lustful Fantasies** - Earlier I mentioned the use of python's blood in project of lust.
- **Depression** - Sadness and heavy feeling of despair.

It is vital to know that some of these afflictions may be a result of one's personal lifestyle, or of reaping what one has sown (Galatians 6:5-9). All those who are enemies of God's children or workers of darkness must of necessity reap afflictions as rewards. Only a change of heart and having a personal relationship with God through Jesus Christ can deliver one from such evil consequences. However, those suffering afflictions projected by the wicked ones can only achieve deliverance by using the Blood and Name of Jesus to counteract the satanic decrees.

In the spiritual realm, once decrees are uttered through blood sacrifices and enchantments, they can be cancelled only through substitution. This is because demonic decrees can never be changed (Esther 8:8 and Daniel 8:15). The penalties or effects of such decrees can be substituted. That is why the scriptures say that the wicked shall be a ransom for the righteous (Proverbs 21:18). For example, Haman had a death sentence decree signed by King Ahasuerus against Mordecai and the Jews. But when Mordecai and Esther's people fasted and prayed for three days, the decree was turned against Haman and his people (Esther 3:8-15; Esther 4:14-17 and Esther 7:1-10).

Also, when Daniel refused to comply with King Darius' decree that was contrary to his belief, and was later thrown in the lion's den, the lions could not devour him because God closed their mouths. However, the men that accused Daniel were later thrown into the den of the lions and were all devoured (Daniel 6:1-28). The men died in place of Daniel because the decree of death had been passed. Even though the men thrown into the lions' den had not committed the offence Daniel was accused of, they had to die in his stead. The scripture says

"The righteous is delivered out of trouble, and the wicked cometh in his stead." (Proverbs 11:8).

In other cases, the wicked can die in anticipation of the righteous. When Shadrach, Meshach and Abednego were thrown into the furnace because of the decree signed by King Nebuchadnezzar, the flame of the fire had already slain some of the king's men who had taken them up for the furnace of fire execution (Daniel 3:15-30). So the king's men died ahead of those Hebrew men, and the fire 'refused' to consume the three Hebrew men who believed in their God. These are perfect examples of the manifestations of the law of substitution's implementation.

The scripture says that those who know their God shall be strong and do exploits (Daniel

11:32b), and God told Job:

> *"Thou shalt also decree a thing, and it shall be established..."* (Job 22:28).

One can turn unrighteous decrees of the wicked ones on their heads by activating Revelations 12:11:

> *"And they overcame him by the blood of the Lamb, and by the word of their testimony."*

This means you can use the Blood of Jesus to nullify satanic decrees which speak against your blessings, or use the Blood of Jesus with the Word of your Testimony (desired expectations)

to establish what you want. The scripture says:

> *"Death and life are in the power of the tongue: and they that love it shall eat the fruit thereof."* (Proverbs 18:21).

The next chapter provides an opportunity for you to use the words of God as framework to establish what you desire, and cancel any unrighteous decrees the enemies or adversaries may have invoked against you and your beloved ones.

CHAPTER 7 - PRAYER POINTS

CONFESSIONS

Confession of sins is very important before going to God in prayers, because sin can prevent our prayers from being answered. In Romans 3:23, the bible says: *"For all have sinned, and come short of the glory of God"*; It is therefore imperative to confess every known and unknown sin as we come to God in prayers.

1 — Isaiah 59:1-2

Behold, the LORD's hand is not shortened, that it cannot save; neither his ear heavy, that it cannot hear: (59:2) But your iniquities have separated between you and your God, and your sins have hid his face from you, that he will not hear.

O Lord my God, I confess all my sins and ask for your forgiveness and cleanse me from all unrighteousness in Jesus Name, Amen.

2 — Revelation 12:11

And they overcame him by the blood of the Lamb, and by the word of their testimony; and they loved not their lives unto the death.

O Lord my God, I cover myself in the blood of Jesus Christ and I confess that the blood of Jesus Christ has rendered powerless satanic or demonic blood sacrifices speaking against my destiny or my future in my life in Jesus' Name, Amen.

FOUNDATIONS

As we mentioned above, every blood, whether it is human or the blood of animals, has a voice. Some people's foundations are polluted by the ritualistic blood connections or covenants of the ancients, forefathers, fathers, parents, husbands, wives or relatives. It is therefore necessary to nullify the voices of these blood sacrifices speaking in our foundation before we may actualize God's destinies for our lives. It is essential at the beginning of this prayer exercise to nullify and silence every other blood crying in your foundation.

3 Psalms 11:3

If the foundations be destroyed, what can the righteous do?

O Lord my God, let every foundation of satanic or demonic blood in my family line be destroyed by the blood of Jesus, in Jesus' Name, Amen.

4 2 Corinthians 6:14

Be ye not unequally yoked together with unbelievers: for what fellowship hath righteousness with unrighteousness? And what communion hath light with darkness?

O Lord my God, I use the blood of Jesus Christ to separate myself from my forefathers' ritualistic covenants in Jesus' Name, Amen.

5 *And Moses took the blood, and sprinkled it on the people, and said, Behold the blood of the covenant, which the LORD hath made with you concerning all these words.*

Exodus 24:8

O Lord my God, I plead the blood of Jesus over my life and I reject demonic blood dedications in my foundation in Jesus' Name, Amen.

BINDING AND RELEASING

Jesus clearly stated in Matthew 12:29: *"Or else how can one enter into a strong man's house, and spoil his goods, except he first bind the strong man? and then he will spoil his house." (Matthew 12:29).* The Blood of Jesus is an effective instrument in binding or releasing demonic spirits that are activated by demonic blood offerings.

6 *And Balaam said unto Balak, Build me here seven altars, and prepare me here seven oxen and seven rams.*

Numbers 23:1

O Lord my God, blood altars erected by my forefathers still speaking evil, I use the blood of Jesus to silence their voices forever in Jesus' Name, Amen.

7 **Ephesians 6:12**

For we wrestle not against flesh and blood, but against principalities, against powers, against the rulers of the darkness of this world, against spiritual wickedness in high places.

O Lord my God, heavenly demons and wicked spirits that demand human blood assigned against me and my family members, be bound and be paralysed in Jesus' Name, Amen.

8 **Jeremiah 44:19**

And when we burned incense to the queen of heaven, and poured out drink offerings unto her, did we make her cakes to worship her, and pour out drink offerings unto her, without our men?

O Lord my God, I use the blood of Jesus Christ to neutralize the activities of the queen of heaven that may demand affliction of our blood in Jesus' Name, Amen.

9 **1 Samuel 28:13**

And the king said unto her, Be not afraid: for what sawest thou? And the woman said unto Saul, I saw gods ascending out of the earth.

O Lord my God, earthly demons and wicked spirits that demand human blood, are hereby bound and rendered powerless concerning me and my family members, in Jesus' Name, Amen.

10

Exodus 20:4

Thou shalt not make unto thee any graven image, or any likeness of any thing that is in heaven above, or that is in the earth beneath, or that is in the water under the earth.

O Lord my God, graven image altars of anything that is in the heaven above, in the earth beneath and in the waters, meant to demand our blood, have been paralysed by the blood of Jesus Christ, Amen.

11

Exodus 20:24

An altar of earth thou shalt make unto me, and shalt sacrifice thereon thy burnt offerings, and thy peace offerings, thy sheep, and thine oxen: in all places where I record my name I will come unto thee, and I will bless thee.

O Lord my God, altars of the earth, in the T-junctions, roundabouts, market-squares, evil forests and on the highways meant to activate of blood sucking demons have been rendered powerless by the blood of Jesus Christ, Amen.

12

Ezekiel 43:19

And thou shalt give to the priests the Levites that be of the seed of Zadok, which approach unto me, to minister unto me, saith the Lord GOD, a young bullock for a sin offering.

O Lord my God, every ordinances of the satanic altars speaking against me as a result of demonic sacrifices, I use the blood of Jesus Christ to nullify them in Jesus' Name, Amen.

13 **Colossians 2:14**

Blotting out the handwriting of ordinances that was against us, which was contrary to us, and took it out of the way, nailing it to his cross

O Lord my God, I use the blood of Jesus Christ to cancel outright demonic handwriting of ordinances that was against us and contrary to God's plan for our lives in Jesus' Name, Amen.

14 **Matthew 12:29**

Or else how can one enter into a strong man's house, and spoil his goods, except he first bind the strong man? and then he will spoil his house.

O Lord my God, every strongman or woman that uses blood for demonic purposes who is a hindrance in my life, I use the blood of Jesus to bind and paralyse you in Jesus' Name, Amen.

15 **Exodus 3:8**

And I am come down to deliver them out of the hand of the Egyptians, and to bring them up out of that land unto a good land and a large, unto a land flowing with milk and honey; unto the place of the Canaanites, and the Hittites, and the Amorites, and the Perizzites, and the Hivites, and the Jebusites.

O Lord my God, I use the blood of Jesus Christ to paralyse the activities of spiritual taskmasters that are using satanic sacrifices to hinder our breakthrough and success in Jesus' Name, Amen.

16 *Matthew 10:36*

And a man's foes shall be they of his own household.

O Lord my God, I use the blood of Jesus Christ to paralyse household enemies that feed on blood in Jesus' Name, Amen.

17 *Isaiah 49:26*

And I will feed them that oppress thee with their own flesh; and they shall be drunken with their own blood, as with sweet wine: and all flesh shall know that I the LORD am thy Saviour and thy Redeemer, the mighty One of Jacob.

O Lord my God, let the blood of Jesus Christ cause all those who wish to drink our blood to be drunken in their own blood in Jesus' Name, Amen.

18 *Ezekiel 35:6*

Therefore, as I live, saith the Lord GOD, I will prepare thee unto blood, and blood shall pursue thee: sith thou hast not hated blood, even blood shall pursue thee.

O Lord my God, all those that use human, animal or bird blood for satanic manipulations and enchantments against me, because I and my family members are under the Blood of Jesus Christ, the blood being used has turned against them in Jesus' Name, Amen.

19 **Hebrews 9:19**

For when Moses had spoken every precept to all the people according to the law, he took the blood of calves and of goats, with water, and scarlet wool, and hyssop, and sprinkled both the book, and all the people

O Lord my God, I use the blood of Jesus Christ to silence blood voices in our forefathers' foundations in Jesus' Name, Amen.

20 **Genesis 37:31**

And they took Joseph's coat, and killed a kid of the goats, and dipped the coat in the blood;

O Lord my God, anyone that has ever used the blood of animal upon gifts and garments for satanic hindrances and manipulations, I use the blood of Jesus to neutralize their evil plans, in Jesus' Name, Amen.

21 **Proverbs 6:17**

A proud look, a lying tongue, and hands that shed innocent blood

O Lord my God, hands that shed innocent blood upon my life, let them be paralysed in Jesus' Name, Amen.

22 *And when it was day, certain of the Jews banded together, and bound themselves under a curse, saying that they would neither eat nor drink till they had killed Paul*

Acts 23:12

O Lord my God, wherever and whenever people have gathered together with blood oath to destroy me, the Blood of Jesus Christ has brought judgment upon them in Jesus' Name, Amen.

23 *And the LORD spake unto Moses, Say unto Aaron, Take thy rod, and stretch out thine hand upon the waters of Egypt, upon their streams, upon their rivers, and upon their ponds, and upon all their pools of water, that they may become blood; and that there may be blood throughout all the land of Egypt, both in vessels of wood, and in vessels of stone.*

Exodus 7:19

O Lord my God, any man or woman that will use occultic blood sacrifices to contend with me, I cover him, his hand, business, home, family and altars with the Blood of Jesus Christ, in Jesus' Name, Amen.

24 *And he shall kill it on the side of the altar northward before the LORD: and the priests, Aaron's sons, shall sprinkle his blood round about upon the altar.*

Leviticus 1:11

O Lord my God, any man or woman that will use human, animal, creeping things or birds' blood to sprinkle at my gates or doors of success or promotion, let the blood of Jesus Christ overthrow their satanic intentions in Jesus' Name, Amen.

25 *The good man is perished out of the earth: and there is none upright among men: they all lie in wait for blood; they hunt every man his brother with a net.*

Micah 7:2

O Lord my God, all they that lie in wait for our blood, have been paralysed by the Blood of Jesus Christ, in Jesus' Name, Amen.

26 *Her young ones also suck up blood: and where the slain are, there is she.*

Job 39:30

O Lord my God, demonized young ones that suck innocent blood have been paralysed by the blood of Jesus Christ, Amen.

27 | *As for the living bird, he shall take it, and the cedar wood, and the scarlet, and the hyssop, and shall dip them and the living bird in the blood of the bird that was killed over the running water*

Leviticus 14:6

O Lord my God, any man or woman that will use the blood of the fowl of the air for satanic manipulation against my progress, I use the Blood of Jesus Christ to render their divinations and enchantments useless in Jesus' Name, Amen.

28 | *The words of the wicked are to lie in wait for blood: but the mouth of the upright shall deliver them.*

Proverbs 12:6

O Lord my God, words of the wicked that lay in wait for my blood, are hereby nullified by the reason of the Blood of Jesus Christ, in Jesus' Name, Amen.

DECREE AND DECLARE

As we mention, what govern the spirit realm are decrees and commands. And the Blood of Jesus is above every other blood. We can use it as a seal of authority in decreeing and declaring the will of God.

29 **Acts 19:12**

So that from his body were brought unto the sick handkerchiefs or aprons, and the diseases departed from them, and the evil spirits went out of them.

O Lord my God, afflictions and diseases occasioned by satanic blood enchantments, I use the Blood of Jesus to command you out, in Jesus' Name, Amen.

30 **Matthew 18:18**

Verily I say unto you, Whatsoever ye shall bind on earth shall be bound in heaven: and whatsoever ye shall loose on earth shall be loosed in heaven.

O Lord my God, I use the Blood of Jesus Christ to decree and bind satanic and demonic spirits assigned against me and my family members in Jesus' Name, Amen.

31 **Exodus 24:8**

And Moses took the blood, and sprinkled it on the people, and said, Behold the blood of the covenant, which the LORD hath made with you concerning all these words.

O Lord my God, I decree and declare that blood of animals in my foundations, have been neutralized and replaced with the Blood of Jesus Christ, in Jesus' Name, Amen.

32 **1 Samuel 26:20**

Now therefore, let not my blood fall to the earth before the face of the LORD: for the king of Israel is come out to seek a flea, as when one doth hunt a partridge in the mountains

O Lord my God, because we are under the Blood of Jesus Christ, our family members' blood will not fall to the earth in Jesus' Name, Amen.

33 **Psalms 106:38**

And shed innocent blood, even the blood of their sons and of their daughters, whom they sacrificed unto the idols of Canaan: and the land was polluted with blood.

O Lord my God, our ancestral lands or properties that have been polluted as a result of human or animal blood sacrifices, I use the Blood of Jesus Christ to redeem them in Jesus' Name, Amen.

34 **Leviticus 20:27**

A man also or woman that hath a familiar spirit, or that is a wizard, shall surely be put to death: they shall stone them with stones: their blood shall be upon them.

O Lord my God, I decree and declare, let the blood of the witches and wizards after our success and promotion be upon their own head, in Jesus' Name, Amen.

35 **Psalms 59:2**

Deliver me from the workers of iniquity, and save me from bloody men.

O Lord my God, I decree that the Blood of Jesus Christ has redeemed me and my family members from bloody men in Jesus' Name, Amen.

36 **Ephesians 1:7**

In whom we have redemption through his blood, the forgiveness of sins, according to the riches of his grace

O Lord my God, I decree and declare that the Blood of Jesus Christ has redeemed me and my family members from our former idolatrous foundations in Jesus' Name, Amen.

37 **Romans 3:15**

Their feet are swift to shed blood:

O Lord my God, I decree and declare, that the feet of those who are swift or anxious to shed blood, be paralysed by the Blood of Jesus, in Jesus' Name, Amen.

38 **Habakkuk 2:17**

For the violence of Lebanon shall cover thee, and the spoil of beasts, which made them afraid, because of men's blood, and for the violence of the land, of the city, and of all that dwell therein.

O Lord my God, I decree and declare that from today, any human, animal or fowl of the air blood that has been promoting violence in our lives, has been nullified by the Blood of Jesus Christ, in Jesus' Name, Amen.

39 **Hebrews 12:24**

And to Jesus the mediator of the new covenant, and to the blood of sprinkling, that speaketh better things that that of Abel.

O Lord my God, I decree and declare that the blood foundations of our forefathers have been destroyed, and that Jesus Christ's blood is our new foundation which is speaking for us in Jesus' Name, Amen.

40 **Revelations 12:11**

And they overcame him by the blood of the Lamb, and by the word of their testimony; and they loved not their lives unto the death.

O Lord my God, I decree and declare that the Blood of Jesus has overcome satanic and demonic bloods fighting our promotion in Jesus' Name, Amen.

41 **Psalms 24:7**

Lift up your heads, O ye gates; and be ye lift up, ye everlasting doors; and the King of glory shall come in.

O Lord my God, I use the Blood of Jesus Christ to decree and declare that blood pillars erected against our promotion and success are hereby destroyed in Jesus' Name, Amen.

42 *And he shall cleanse the house with the blood of the bird, and with the running water, and with the living bird, and with the cedar wood, and with the hyssop, and with the scarlet*

Leviticus 14:52

O Lord my God, I decree and declare that the Blood of Jesus Christ has silenced blood of birds sacrificed to the powers in the water that are crying against me and my family members in Jesus' Name, Amen.

43 *And Jesus answered and said unto him, Blessed art thou, Simon Barjona: for flesh and blood hath not revealed it unto thee, but my Father which is in heaven.*

Matthew 16:17

O Lord my God, I use the Blood of Jesus Christ to decree and declare that flesh and blood will never reveal my secrets to powers of darkness in Jesus' Name, Amen.

44 *There were present at that season some that told him of the Galileans, whose blood Pilate had mingled with their sacrifices.*

Luke 13:1

O Lord my God, any food, drink, presents, gifts, money and other items mingled with demonic blood that have contact with me is nullified by the Blood of Jesus Christ, in Jesus' Name, Amen.

45

John 6:54

Whoso eateth my flesh, and drinketh my blood, hath eternal life; and I will raise him up at the last day.

O Lord my God, I decree and declare that as I eat the flesh and drink the Blood of Jesus Christ, I have a covenant of life with Him forever, in Jesus' Name, Amen.

46

Isaiah 49:25

But thus saith the LORD, Even the captives of the mighty shall be taken away, and the prey of the terrible shall be delivered: for I will contend with him that contendeth with thee, and I will save thy children.

O Lord my God, I decree and declare, those contending with me and my family members by using demonized blood, let the Blood of Jesus Christ contend with them in Jesus' Name, Amen.

47

1 Kings 20:41

And he hasted, and took the ashes away from his face; and the king of Israel discerned him that he was of the prophets.

O Lord my God, anyone that has taken satanic ashes and mixed them with demonized blood to cover my face, I use the Blood of Jesus Christ to cleanse my face, and I decree and declare that those involved have perished in Jesus' Name, Amen.

48

Numbers 23:23

Surely there is no enchantment against Jacob, neither is there any divination against Israel: according to this time it shall be said of Jacob and of Israel, What hath God wrought!

O Lord my God, anyone that has used or will use our picture and sprinkle demonized blood to invoke negative aura upon our lives, I use the Blood of Jesus Christ to nullify their evil projections, in Jesus' Name, Amen.

49

Lamentations 3:12

He hath bent his bow, and set me as a mark for the arrow.

O Lord my God, whosoever has used satanic blood to place evil marks upon our faces, house, business premises, cars, etc. I use the Blood of Jesus Christ to cancel such evil marks in Jesus' Name, Amen.

50

Isaiah 54:15

Behold, they shall surely gather together, but not by me: whosoever shall gather together against thee shall fall for thy sake.

O Lord my God, whenever blood drinkers will gather against me and my family members, let the Blood of Jesus Christ scatter them, in Jesus' Name, Amen.

51 **Isaiah 43:19**

Behold, I will do a new thing; now it shall spring forth; shall ye not know it? I will even make a way in the wilderness, and rivers in the desert.

O Lord my God, wherever they have used satanic blood offering to stop my progress or moving forward, I use the Blood of Jesus Christ to open every closed way, in Jesus' Name, Amen.

52 **Exodus 29:15**

Thou shalt also take one ram; and Aaron and his sons shall put their hands upon the head of the ram.

O Lord my God, wherever they have celebrated demonic blood sacrifices in order to hinder me and my family members, I use the Blood of Jesus Christ to frustrate their plans, in Jesus' Name, Amen.

53 **Psalms 121:6**

The sun shall not smite thee by day, nor the moon by night.

O Lord my God, anywhere our names have been written on a paper and sprinkled with demonized blood, and divinations are being made to powers in the sun, moon and stars, let the Blood of Jesus Christ answer them, in Jesus' Name, Amen.

54 **Acts 7:59**

And they stoned Stephen, calling upon God, and saying, Lord Jesus, receive my spirit.

O Lord my God, anyone that have used stones and mixed them with demonized blood and thrown them into our compound for afflictions, let the Blood of Jesus Christ render useless such actions in Jesus' Name, Amen.

55 **Jeremiah 46:10**

For this is the day of the Lord GOD of hosts, a day of vengeance, that he may avenge him of his adversaries: and the sword shall devour, and it shall be satiate and made drunk with their blood: for the Lord GOD of hosts hath a sacrifice in the north country by the river Euphrates.

O Lord my God, let every sworn adversaries of our destiny that have ever used demonized blood to fight against us, be drunken in their own blood in Jesus' Name, Amen.

56 **Jeremiah 1:13**

And the word of the LORD came unto me the second time, saying, What seest thou? And I said, I see a seething pot; and the face thereof is toward the north.

O Lord my God, anywhere they have used satanic pots filled with demonized blood to raise an altar against my success, I use the Blood of Jesus Christ to render useless their evil enchantments and divinations in Jesus' Name, Amen.

57

Proverbs 3:23

Then shalt thou walk in thy way safely, and thy foot shall not stumble.

O Lord my God, anyone that will ever use our footprint and mingle the sand of it with demonized blood, let the Blood of Jesus hinder them forever in Jesus' Name, Amen.

58

Jeremiah 18:21

Therefore deliver up their children to the famine, and pour out their blood by the force of the sword; and let their wives be bereaved of their children, and be widows; and let their men be put to death; let their young men be slain by the sword in battle.

O Lord my God, those that are monitoring us for evil, let them pour out their blood by force of the heavenly sword in Jesus' Name, Amen.

59

Hebrews 10:4

For it is not possible that the blood of bulls and of goats should take away sins.

O Lord my God, I decree and declare that the blood of bulls, goats, birds and human beings over my success and destiny have been rendered useless by the Blood of Jesus Christ, in Jesus' Name, Amen.